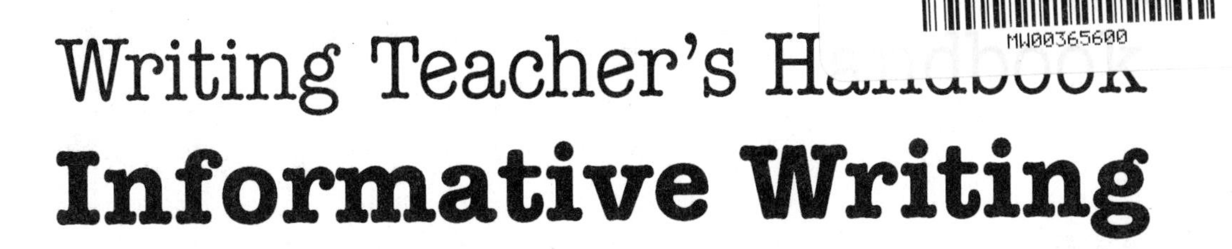

Writing Teacher's Handbook
Informative Writing

Written by June Hetzel and Deborah McIntire

"Like bees who by instinct go from flower to flower gathering honey, writers, merely by being alive, are constantly gathering ideas and impressions—their honey—which eventually will lodge somewhere . . ."
—Eleanor Estes, from a talk given at a meeting of the International Reading Association

Illustrator: Corbin Hillam
Editor: Joel Kupperstein
Project Director: Carolea Williams

Table of Contents

Introduction

Informative Writing is one resource in the *Writing Teacher's Handbook* four-book series that assists teachers of grades 4–6 in effectively implementing classroom writing programs. The lessons in each book include actual writing samples from upper-grade students.

Writing Domains

Each resource book in the *Writing Teacher's Handbook* series describes detailed lessons in one of the four writing domains—narrative, expressive, informative, and persuasive.

The *informative domain* encompasses writing products that state factual information and evidence (e.g., news articles, how-tos).The *persuasive domain* involves convincing readers of beliefs and reasoning (e.g., persuasive essays, campaign speeches). The *narrative domain* focuses on telling a story (e.g., autobiographical incidents, short stories). The *expressive domain* includes poems and stories that express sensory detail and emotions (e.g., journal entries, haiku).

Many writing products fall within more than one domain. For example, a brochure may have the primary purpose of informing people about a national park (informational), but the brochure may also be intended to convince people to visit (persuasive). Emphasize the critical components of each writing product to help your students sharpen their writing skills and prepare them for writing success.

Lesson Plan Format

Lessons in this book include:

Critical Components—a list of the essential components of each writing product

Preparation—a description of what teachers need to do prior to the lesson

Setting the Stage—hints for introducing the lesson and engaging student interest

Instructional Input—directions for initiating a formal writing lesson and modeling the critical components of writing samples

Guided Practice—exercises for reinforcing the writing lesson

Independent Practice—activities to help students write independently

Presentation—ideas for organizing, publishing, and presenting student work

Teaching Hints/Extensions—tips to extend and explore the topic and writing domain

In addition, at the end of each section is a reproducible rubric for evaluating student work. Give students the rubric at the beginning of the lesson so they can write with specific goals in mind.

The Writing Process

The writing process involves five steps: prewriting, writing a rough draft, revising, editing, and publishing/presenting the final product. These five steps are integral to any type of writing and form the foundation for all writing lessons in this book. Guide students through the stages of the process for each writing lesson, particularly the activities in the Independent Practice sections. Emphasize to students that they may need to repeat the cycle of revising and editing several times until their manuscript is ready for publication. Provide students with copies of the Writing Process Cards (page 13), and have them complete a card for each writing task and attach it to the final product. The first space for check-off in the Editing box of the Writing Process Card is for self-editing and the second is for peer or teacher editing.

Prewriting

Prewriting occurs after a thorough discussion of a topic but before formal writing about the topic. The prewriting stage is a structured brainstorming session aimed at eliciting spontaneous thinking about a specific topic. For the informative domain, research about a topic may occur before, during, and after prewriting activities. During the prewriting stage, help students use clusters and graphic organizers to organize ideas and facts.

For example, prewriting for a paragraph on Yosemite Valley might include a simple cluster such as the following:

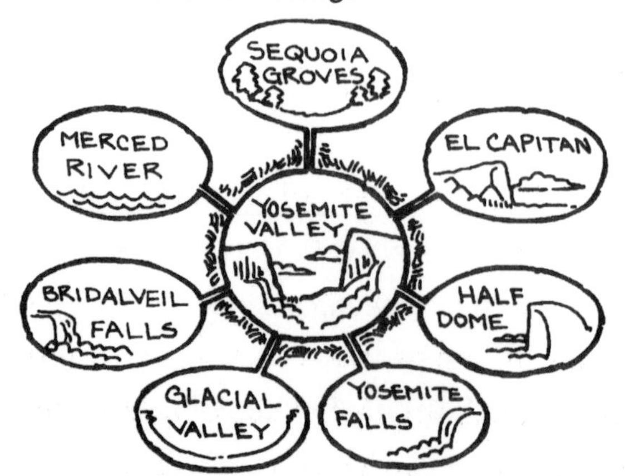

The central idea, Yosemite Valley, becomes the subject of the topic sentence while ideas in the spokes are expressed in the topic sentence.

Yosemite Valley has many prominent features, including the Merced River, sequoia groves, and numerous mountains and waterfalls.

The content of the cluster's spokes becomes the basis for supporting sentences:

The most prominent feature of Yosemite Valley is the Merced River, which runs about seven miles through the center of this glacial valley. Throughout the valley, one can view various sequoia groves, such as the Merced, Tuolumne, and Mariposa groves. Prominent mountains surrounding the valley include El Capitan and Half Dome. The most prominent waterfalls viewed from the south entrance include Bridalveil Falls and the spectacular Yosemite Falls.

All of the lessons in this book involve informative writing. This, of course, means that students must gather factual information. In each lesson, students are challenged to write direct, succinct, and accurate accounts of factual information with style and content that engages and motivates the reader.

Throughout this book, you will find writing frames that help students organize their thinking and include the critical components of each writing product. This will help provide structure for each piece of informative writing during the prewriting stage.

After students complete the brainstorming prewriting session, have them skim over their work and trim unnecessary or irrelevant content. The remaining information forms the skeleton or framework of the project.

Rough Draft

The rough draft is the first round of organized writing. During rough-draft writing, students write spontaneously, following the organizational framework of the prewriting graphic organizer. Students should feel free to deviate from the skeletal framework of the prewriting organizer, as long as the requirements of the writing type (as defined by the rubric) are met. Frequently, the most effective writing comes from the spontaneity of a rough draft.

Students should not worry about precise spelling and punctuation while writing rough drafts. During the editing stage, however, spelling and punctuation should be fine-tuned to perfection!

Revising

The revising stage requires students to reorganize at four levels: the entire piece, each paragraph, each sentence, and each individual word. Encourage students to revise in this order to save time and, potentially, unnecessary work. For example, if a writer deletes an entire paragraph, no time is wasted revising the sentences or words in that paragraph.

Revising the Entire Piece

At this level of revising, students look at the "big picture." They read and reread their writing, asking the following questions:

Does the piece flow from one idea to another?

Are the paragraphs in a logical sequence?

Are there smooth transitions between paragraphs?

Is the writing clear and understandable?

Are the facts accurate?

Are there unnecessary facts that can be omitted?

Does the writing product meet the requirements of the rubric?

Revising Each Paragraph

In addition to larger organizational revising, students must revise their writing at the paragraph level. At this stage, students carefully examine each paragraph, asking the following:

Are sentences arranged in logical order?

Is there a topic sentence?

Are there supporting sentences?

Are there redundant words, phrases, or ideas?

Does each paragraph add to the clarity, depth, and/or interest of the piece?

Writing Tip

It is common for beginning writers to struggle with the sentence order of a paragraph. Model the following "cut-and-paste" methods to demonstrate how to revise a paragraph.

1. Cut and paste using the computer.
2. Physically cut and paste the text to different sections of the page.
3. Color-code sentences that belong together.

Revising Each Sentence

Students may wish to reorder or revise words within sentences to strengthen preciseness, add interest, and increase the depth of the information.

Weak Example:
The Merced River runs through Yosemite Valley.

Strong Example:
The Merced River snakes through Yosemite Valley in a seven-mile path.

Word efficiency is another aspect of sentence revision. Students should be taught to use as few words as necessary to relay the desired meaning.

> Weak Example:
> **The gray whale has a lot of scars that were caused from animals, such as crustaceans and small whale lice, and though the whale was black at birth, it now appears gray in color.**
>
> Strong Example:
> **Though black at birth, the gray whale, mottled with white scars from crustaceans and whale lice, now has a gray appearance.**

Revising Individual Words

Revising word-by-word constitutes fine tuning. This is the time to have students pull out the thesaurus and dictionary. This is the time to polish!

Here are some tips for revising at the word level:

Use interesting words—

> Weak Example:
> **The redwoods can get 300 feet tall.**
>
> Strong Example:
> **Some towering redwoods stand 300 feet tall.**

Strengthen verbs—

> Weak Example:
> **He got the 200-pound barbell.**
>
> Strong Example:
> **He pressed the 200-pound barbell.**

Clarify pronouns—

> Weak Example:
> **He and I were well-acquainted.**
>
> Strong Example:
> **C.S. Lewis and I were well-acquainted.**

Clarify vague concepts—

> Weak Example:
> **He painted flowers.**
>
> Strong Example:
> **Van Gogh painted irises.**

Use sensory detail to evoke emotion—

> Weak Example:
> **There was a 6.2 earthquake in Whittier.**
>
> Strong Example:
> **The Whittier Narrows quake registered 6.2 and collapsed several structures, as it terrified residents.**

Editing

At the editing stage, students make sure words are spelled correctly and punctuation is accurate. Here are some hints for this ongoing area of growth.

Editing Marks

Photocopy the Editing Marks reproducible (page 14) for students to refer to as they complete this stage of the writing process. Be sure students are familiar with and comfortable using editing symbols before beginning their first writing-process piece.

Spelling

Be sure students keep ongoing personal dictionaries in which they record new words they encounter. Included in these dictionaries should be a list of the most commonly used words in their writing. Also, be sure students have access to comprehensive dictionaries and thesauruses. Reinforce the idea that students may need to repeat the editing stage for a particular writing project.

If your students write using a computer, teach them how to use programs that check spelling. However, be sure that they clearly understand that computers will not detect missing words or homophone errors.

Punctuation

Mastering punctuation can be challenging. Teach punctuation as you teach writing, starting with the basics (ending punctuation and capitalization) and moving to commas, semicolons, and colons as students gain mastery. Do not expect perfection at the rough-draft stage. The goal of teaching writing is to help students improve their writing with each revision.

Repeated Reading

Students often have the misconception that one round of reading is sufficient in editing a piece. Encourage several reads by several people (the author, peers, and adults). Each reading provides an opportunity to improve the writing. For peer editing, students might engage in a round-robin discussion or an "author's chair," where one student reads a piece to the group or class and solicits constructive feedback.

Publishing/Presenting

The most rewarding aspect of the writing process is the final draft, or publishing/presenting stage. At this point, the writer finally sees his or her completed work in polished form, available for others' enjoyment. Provide forums for students to read their writing to one another, to other classes, and to parents. Encourage students to bind their writing into books and submit copies to school and classroom libraries. Students may also want to submit their work to local newspapers for publication. Tape-record stories for reading centers and post students' writing in your classroom on bulletin board displays.

Writing Devices

Certain literary devices can increase the effectiveness and beauty of students' writing. These devices include alliteration, metaphor, simile, sensory detail, onomatopoeia, and personification. Review these devices throughout your writing lessons, particularly during the revising stage. Challenge students to locate these devices in their independent reading materials.

Alliteration

Increase students' understanding of how alliteration—a string of words with the same initial sound—enhances the "sound" of language. Read and recite classic tongue twisters *(Peter Piper picked a peck of pickled peppers),* make up original tongue twisters *(Rhonda Rhino wrestled raggedy Rita Rhino),* and brainstorm phrases that include repetitive initial sounds *(Sally's savory sweets, Dominating Dominic,* and *Veronica Victor's venom).* Challenge students to complete these alliterative phrases and use alliteration in their writing. The use of alliteration is especially effective in writing such as newspaper article headlines because it draws attention to the article.

Metaphor

Increase students' ability to relay meaning to a reader by comparing two ideas using "word pictures," or metaphors. Read some ordinary sentences and enhance the meaning of the sentences by rewriting them using metaphor.

Weak Example:
The manuscript has a lot of good qualities and can be improved.

Strong Example:
The manuscript is a diamond in the rough.

Weak Example:
The young man is very strong and one day will be in the Olympics.

Strong Example:
Such a young Hercules will one day compete in the Olympics.

Simile

Similar to a metaphor, a simile compares two ideas using *as* or *like.* Help students enjoy similes by reading *Quick As a Cricket* by Audrey Wood. Discuss simile examples in the book, such as "quick as a cricket" and "strong as an ox." Discuss how similes evoke images that enhance the mental pictures of what the writer is trying to relate.

Sensory Detail

Writers who use sensory detail (words and phrases that vividly describe sight, sound, smell, taste, and touch) involve the reader's senses and add interest to their writing.

Weak Example:
I felt hot and tired after the race through the desert.

Strong Example:
Every inch of my body ached after the grueling race through the scorching, arid desert.

Onomatopoeia

Onomatopoeic words represent the sounds of the things they describe, for example, *crunch*, *crackle*, and *bang*. These words help clarify readers' mental images and intensify events and emotions.

Weak Example:
The sound made her shake.

Strong Example:
The crunch beneath her feet sent a tingle up her spine.

Weak Example:
The magician made the object disappear.

Strong Example:
Poof! With a swish of the magician's wand, the object disappeared.

Personification

Personification is the assigning of human characteristics to a nonhuman object. To provide students practice with this device, guide them in brainstorming a list of objects and the human characteristics that could describe them. Then, create sentences using items from this personification list. For example, students might use the word *shy* to describe the moon. Then, they might write the sentence *The moon shyly peeked through the clouds.*

Assessment

Each lesson in this resource includes a rubric for evaluating student work. These rubrics allow readers to assess the critical components, style issues, originality, and mechanics of the work. Some also include space for readers' comments.

Rubrics are valuable tools at all stages of the writing process. Give the rubrics to students as they begin prewriting to help them understand the criteria by which their work will be assessed. At this early stage, rubrics also help students understand the focus and purpose of each writing genre.

As students revise their own work, rubrics help them assess the quality of what they have written. Have students complete a rubric for each draft they write and include detailed comments each time. Also, have peer editors complete rubrics when evaluating classmates' work. Objectively evaluating one's own work is a difficult task, to be sure. Give students practice evaluating each other's work. When students make tactful, constructive comments, they contribute to the improvement of each other's writing.

Rubrics also give you a standardized format for the final assessment of students' writing. Ask students to attach all of their completed rubrics to each project they turn in. Use the student-completed rubrics to assess the progress students made while writing.

When you complete the final rubric and present it to students, they will clearly understand why they received the grades they were given.

As students complete writing projects, you may want to store their work in portfolios. Whether your portfolios are simple file folders in a file cabinet or decorated pizza boxes in which students can store artwork that accompanies their writing, be sure students have open access to them. Invite students to add at any time work they feel shows growth or excellence. Review these portfolios when determining students' writing grades, and have them available for parents to look through at Open House and at parent-teacher conferences.

Writing Process Cards

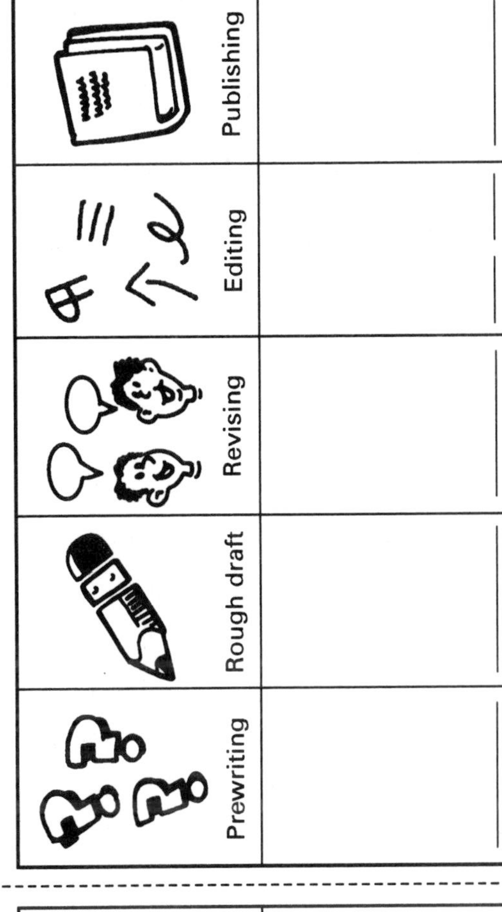

Prewriting	Rough draft	Revising	Editing	Publishing

Directions: Check or initial each stage as you complete it. Attach a completed card to your final draft. Attach your previous work (prewriting, rough draft, revising, and editing pages) behind your final draft to show the stages of your writing process.

Prewriting	Rough draft	Revising	Editing	Publishing

Directions: Check or initial each stage as you complete it. Attach a completed card to your final draft. Attach your previous work (prewriting, rough draft, revising, and editing pages) behind your final draft to show the stages of your writing process.

Prewriting	Rough draft	Revising	Editing	Publishing

Directions: Check or initial each stage as you complete it. Attach a completed card to your final draft. Attach your previous work (prewriting, rough draft, revising, and editing pages) behind your final draft to show the stages of your writing process.

Prewriting	Rough draft	Revising	Editing	Publishing

Directions: Check or initial each stage as you complete it. Attach a completed card to your final draft. Attach your previous work (prewriting, rough draft, revising, and editing pages) behind your final draft to show the stages of your writing process.

Editing Marks

Editing Mark	Examples in Text	Meaning
≡	watch out!	Capitalize the letter.
/	Come here Quickly.	Use lowercase.
^	Look at that giraffe.	Insert a letter. (This symbol is called a caret.)
⊙	Place a period here	Insert a period.
^	When it rains the geraniums love it.	Insert a comma.
¶	. . . with me. The next day . . .	Start a new paragraph.
" "	Good morning, Sally called.	Insert quotations.
	pop corn	Join words.
	June and and Deborah wrote this book.	Delete this word.
^	Luella and Carolea like it.	Insert a word.
	Can you with come me?	Reverse word order.
#	Make a wise decision.	Insert a space.

News Segment
(Audio/Visual Media)

Critical Components

News segments or "newsbites" are the brief updates on current events (approximately 60–120 words) that compose entire news broadcasts. News segments answer *who, what, where, when,* and *why.* Newsbites avoid repetition and aim for economy of presentation by using concise phrases to deliver precise information.

Preparation

Videotape several brief news segments from the evening news. Focus on subjects of interest to your students. Make overhead tranparencies of pages 18 and 20. Photocopy pages 19, 21, and 22 for students.

Setting the Stage

Play for your class the news segments you recorded. Highlight the fact that each news-bite briefly and concisely presents the most important information. Compare a lengthy, in-depth full-coverage news story or news-paper or magazine article to a news seg-ment. Use the analogy that a full-coverage story is like a full meal, while a news seg-ment is like a bite. Explain to students that this is one reason news segments are often called "newsbites."

Instructional Input

1. Display and discuss the overhead trans-parency of the Key Journalistic Questions (page 18) to familiarize students with the questions usually answered in a news segment.

2. Replay the taped newsbites for the class. As each segment is played, encourage students to identify the answer to each journalistic question. Chart responses on the board.

3. Discuss with students the difficulty of communicating all the important facts in such a brief format. Stress the importance of using precise language that avoids excessive wordiness to ensure clarity and well-crafted, concise phrases.

For example, compare the following two newsbites and discuss which presents the information more clearly and concisely.

Monkey Madness

On Monday evening, May 8th, the people of Wheaton, Illinois, were very shocked when they saw a small little monkey walking down Grant Avenue. The little monkey was having a good time playing in people's yards and making funny sounds and gestures. Suddenly, a huge German Shepherd dog started barking and barking. The monkey got very scared and climbed up a huge oak tree as fast as he could. The people who owned the dog put him in the backyard and called the fire department. They asked the firemen if they rescued monkeys from trees. The firemen finally got the monkey down. It turns out that the monkey lived at the city zoo with its mother. He got out of his cage area by going through two bars that were loose. The bars were loose because of the big storm last week.

Monkey Madness

On Monday evening, May 8th, residents of Wheaton, Illinois, were startled to see a baby monkey strolling down Grant Avenue. The six-week-old primate seemed to be enjoying his outing until he encountered a large German Shepherd. The dog's ferocious barking sent the little fellow scampering up the nearest tree. Alarmed neighbors corralled the dog and contacted the local fire department. Eventually, the baby primate was rescued and returned to his anxious mother at the city zoo. Relieved zoo officials reported that the primate escaped between two iron bars that had been loosened during last week's storm.

4. After discussing the two examples, replay the newsbites you recorded. Elicit from students ways the writer of the second example avoided repeating words and included precise descriptions and concise phrases. Chart this information on the board.

Article	Synonyms	Precise Descriptions	Concise Phrases
Monkey Madness			

Guided Practice

1. Distribute copies of the News Segment Sample (First Draft) on page 19. Invite students to work with a partner in circling and labeling answers to the five key journalistic questions. Discuss responses.

2. Inform students that this is the author's first draft and that it still needs revision. Invite students to work with their partners in eliminating unnecessary words, replacing repeated words with appropriate synonyms, and substituting bland or general words with more precise, colorful descriptions.

3. Encourage students to share their revised news segments. Display the overhead transparency of the News Segment Sample (Final Draft) on page 20. Discuss ways the author's revision was similar and/or different from theirs.

Independent Practice

1. Provide students with copies of the News Segment Frame (page 21). Have them complete the frame and write a rough draft of a one-minute news segment that focuses on a local news or school event.

2. Invite students to collaborate with partners to revise their first drafts and eliminate weak and repetitious sections. Provide students with the News Segment Rubric (page 22), which will assist them.

Presentation

- Have students work in small groups to produce their own news show. Place a table at the front of the room to replicate a news desk. Invite one student to serve as the announcer who introduces the broadcast, and have each student report his or her own story.

- Videotape student news broadcasts that cover class and school functions. Share these videotapes with parents at special events such as Open House or Back-to-School Night.

- Have students write news scripts and produce a news broadcast about a historic period. Consider intermingling historical skits with newsbites from the same historical time period. For example, *We interrupt this episode of* As the Colonies Turn *with an important newsbreak. . . . It has been reported that Paul Revere was seen riding about the countryside bearing enlightening news!*

Teaching Hints and Extensions

- Contact a local radio or television station and request that the news department save a day's worth of teletype news reports from news services. Since used teletype printouts are discarded, most stations are happy to save them for schools if they are picked up promptly. Encourage students to write news segments based on the raw data on the teletype printout.

- Provide practice in concise summarizing. Encourage students to bring in articles of interest. Then, have them summarize the article in decreasing lengths. For example, if students bring in a 500-word article, ask them to summarize the article in 100 words, then 80 words, then 60 words, and finally, 50 words.

Key Journalistic Questions

A reporter always seeks to answer these key journalistic questions.

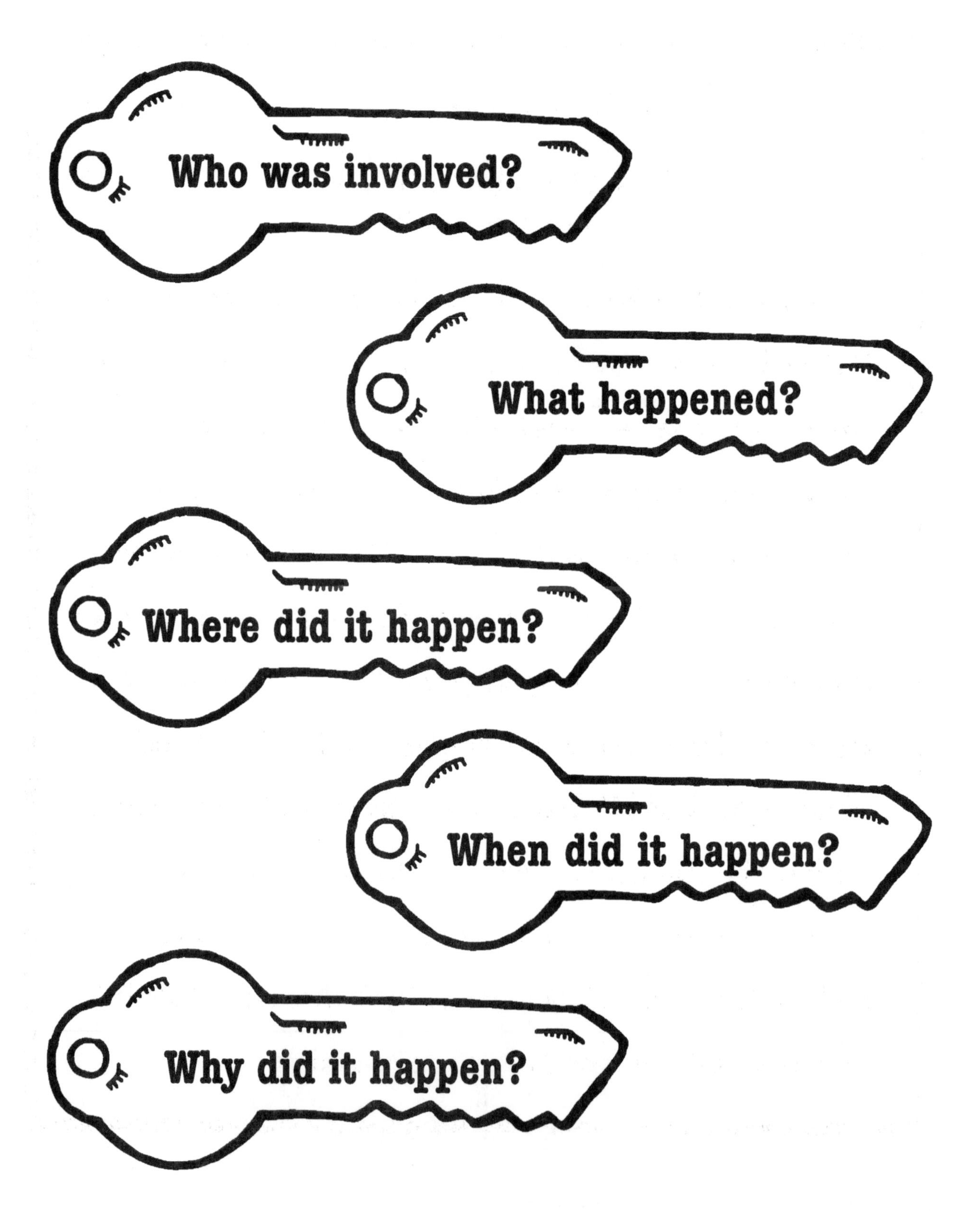

Name: ______________________________

News Segment Sample
(First Draft)

Directions: Circle and label the answers to the key journalistic questions *Who, What, Where, When,* and *Why.*

• Saved by a Scream •

Student Author: Chelsea Stough

One Saturday afternoon, a young girl from Yorba Linda named Chelsea Stough was saved by her screaming ability. Chelsea said it started because she was bored. All day she kept trying to think of things to do. Finally, she thought about climbing her neighbor's tree. She was a little scared but she decided to climb all the way to the top anyway. After having fun at the top, Chelsea decided to climb down, but a scary thing happened. Her long blond hair was caught on a branch and she was hanging in midair. She started screaming her head off. Luckily, her brother heard her and rescued her from the near-accident. When she was safe, Chelsea said, "I ran into my house and put ice-cold water on my hot, burning head." Asked if she'd climb a tree again, Chelsea said, "Only if I tie back my hair and keep my vocal chords in shape."

News Segment Sample
(Final Draft)

• Saved by a Scream •

by Chelsea Stough

On Saturday, September 10th, Chelsea Stough, an adventurous eleven-year-old from Yorba Linda, was saved by her loud scream. Chelsea reported that her adventure began when she decided to alleviate her boredom by climbing a neighbor's tree. After the thrill of the climb, she began her descent. Suddenly, her long blond hair got caught on a branch, leaving her dangling in midair. She began to scream loud and long. Luckily, her brother heard her scream and ran to free her. Asked if she'd ever climb a tree again, Chelsea replied, "Only if I tie back my hair and keep my vocal chords in shape."

Name: ______________________________

News Segment Frame

Directions:

1. Choose a news event of interest to you.
2. Answer in the shapes below the five journalistic questions regarding the event.
3. Develop a first draft of a 60-second news segment script, incorporating your answers to the five journalistic questions.
4. Revise and edit your rough draft.
5. Write a final draft.

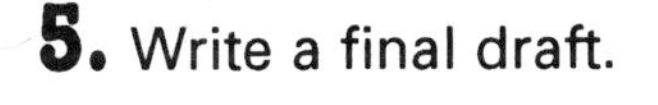

WHEN?

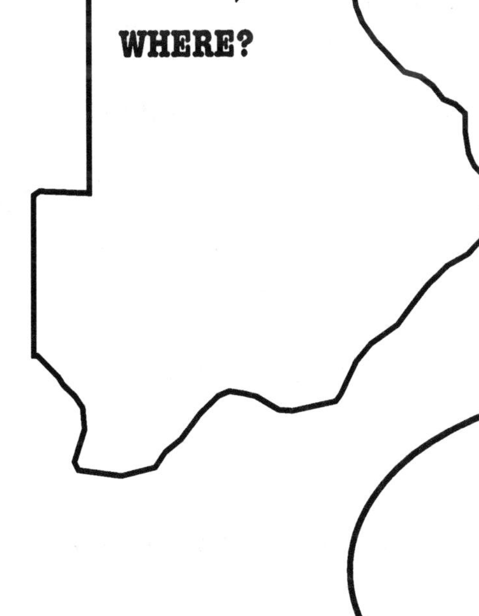

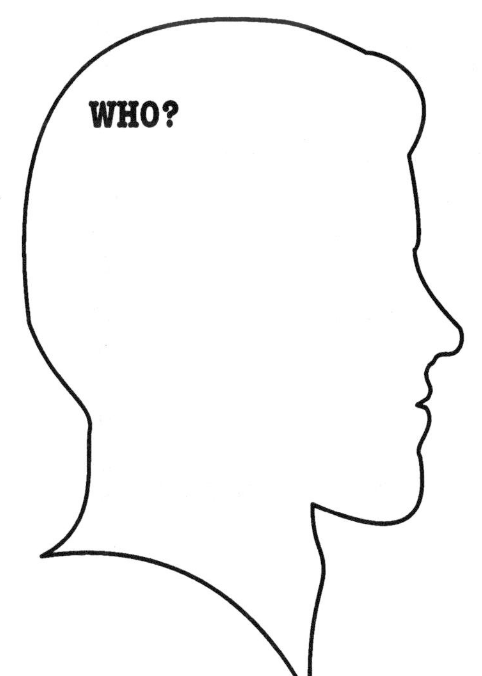

WHY?

WHAT?

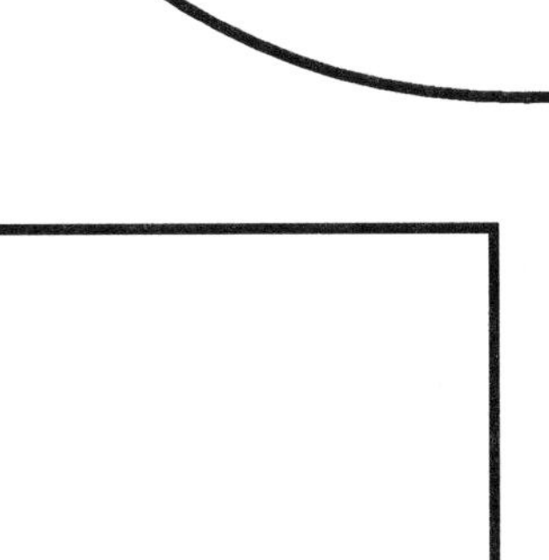

Writer's Name: ______________________ Evaluator's Name: ______________________

News Segment Rubric

	Great!	O.K.	Needs Help
Critical Components			
Updates reader on a current event			
Short and concise (60–120 words)			
Answers *who, what, where, when,* and *why*			
Avoids repetition			
Includes precise descriptions and concise phrases			
Style			
Word Choice			
Strong, active verbs			
Precise words			
Words that evoke imagery and sensory detail			
Coherence			
Clearly presented ideas			
Logically sequenced ideas			
Originality			
Mechanics			
Ending punctuation			
Capitalization			
Comma rules			
Quotation marks			
Paragraph structure			

Comments

____

____

____

News Article
(Print Media)

Critical Components

News articles include a headline or title that describes the content and grabs the reader's attention. News articles include the writer's name in a byline that follows the headline. News articles answer *who, what, where, when,* and *why.* News articles present the most important information in the first paragraph, followed by less important facts and more specific details. News articles inform the reader about the sources of the facts (for example, *According to the Orange County Animal Shelter . . .).*

Preparation

Ask students to bring to class several current news articles. Bring several articles from your own newspaper. Make overhead transparencies of pages 18, 26, and 28. Photocopy pages 27, 29, and 30 for students.

Setting the Stage

Start the lesson by displaying the newspaper to which you subscribe and read regularly. Explain the features of this newspaper and summarize a few interesting articles you have read in the last week. Finally, divide the class into small groups and give each group a different news article (one you or a student brought to class). Invite groups to read their articles to find the main idea.

Instructional Input

1. Display and discuss the overhead transparency of the Key Journalistic Questions (page 18). Have students reread their articles and record the answers to the questions on the transparency. Allow time for groups to share their findings with the class.

2. Display the overhead transparency of page 26 *(Writing Like the Pros).* Read and discuss the inverted-triangle organization technique. Invite the groups to evaluate their articles to see if they fit this pattern.

Guided Practice

1. Distribute copies of the News Article Sample (First Draft) found on page 27 and the News Article Rubric found on page 30. Have students read the article with partners and answer the questions that follow. Ask students to make revision recommendations based on the rubric's criteria.

2. Discuss students' revision recommendations. Then display the overhead transparency of the News Article Sample (Final Draft) found on page 28. Discuss the revisions the author made and how these revisions strengthen the article. (Be sure to review the critical components of a news article.) Highlight the fact that the author contacted the Orange County Animal Shelter to include important follow-up information that would be helpful to her readers. In sharing this information, she included her source.

3. Explain to students that ending an article can be challenging. Some options for writing a closing include making a connection to the opening line, making a recommendation to the reader, or restating the thesis or topic of the article.

Independent Practice

1. Invite students to complete the News Article Frame (page 29). Students may wish to report on something that has happened to them, a friend, or a family member. If students choose to write about someone else, be sure they have that person's permission. Discuss with students the ethics of reporting news and make them aware of issues such as libel, slander, and plagiarism.

2. Have students use their completed frame to develop a news article.

3. Ask students to edit and revise their article using the News Article Rubric (page 30).

Presentation

- Combine student articles into a newspaper titled *The Room __ Times.* Keep in mind that students may need to work on their articles for several days to compile, design, and produce this publication. Invite students to serve on one of the following teams in the production of the newspaper.

Editor(s)-in-Chief: responsible for the final product; coordinates all editors
Layout Editor(s): analyzes where to place each story in the paper and determines the graphic layout of the articles, headlines, and other features
Photographer(s)/Artist(s): provides photos or illustrations that accompany articles
Copy Editor(s): proofreads all text for correct spelling and punctuation
Mechanical Department: selects the production method for the newspaper and oversees its production
Distribution Department: decides who receives copies, how many copies should be printed, and how the newspaper will be delivered

Teaching Hints/Extensions

- Expand this lesson to include ethical concerns. Discuss how news articles may be biased or poorly supported by facts. Discuss how content and word choice give the media influential power. For example, each of the following pairs of descriptions describes the same person. Ask students how the word selections in each description might influence a reader's opinion.

  The ordinary girl versus *The poorly clad girl*

  Her face, masked in heavy makeup versus *Her scars, covered with makeup*

  The suspicious-looking man snuck into the building versus *The tall, dignified gentleman quietly walked into the building*

- Set up a newspaper study and reference center. At first, include school newspapers and newsletters, and then expand it by including newspapers from your community. Most newspapers offer classrooms free copies or charge only a nominal fee.

- Contrast informative and expressive writing by explaining that expressive writing includes descriptive passages and small details while informative writing presents facts briefly and succinctly. Discuss the justifications for each style, and describe instances when each domain is advantageous or appropriate.

- Invite students to write a newspaper article that details an event studied in history, such as Paul Revere's Ride or the assassination of Julius Caesar.

- Invite students to publish a historical newspaper that covers news events from the time period studied in a particular location (for example, *The Salem Gazette* or *The Boston Herald*).

Writing Like the Pros

This style of writing is referred to as the Inverted Triangle. This is an effective writing technique for reporters because readers often skim the daily newspaper, reading only the titles, picture captions, and first paragraphs of each article. Include the most important information at the top of the Inverted Triangle and the less important details at the bottom.

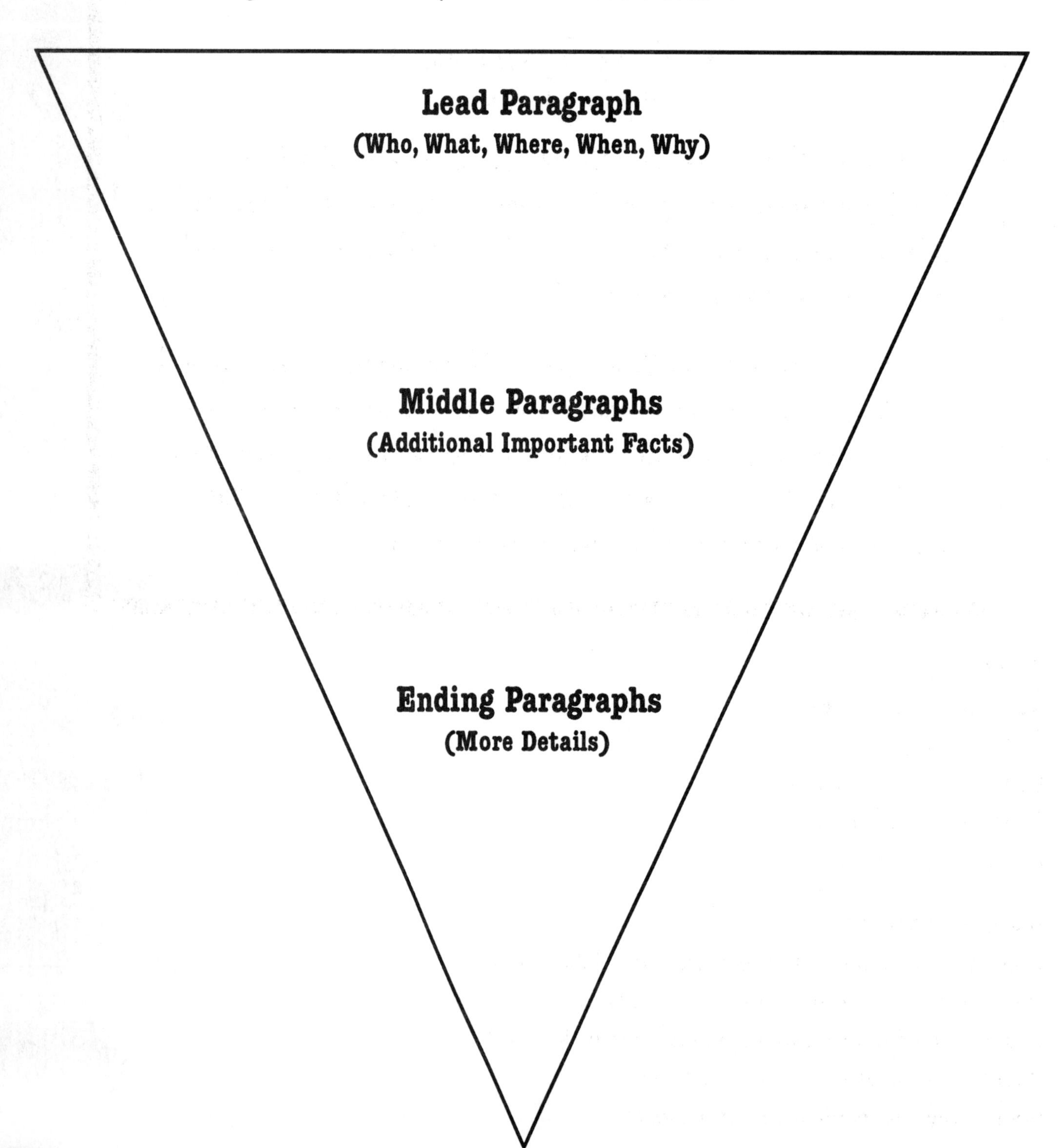

Name: ______________________________

News Article Sample
(First Draft)

Directions: Read the first draft and, on a separate sheet of paper, answer the journalistic questions and make recommendations for revisions.

• Baby Opossums •

Student Author: Stephanie Hachey

Cynthia Hachey walked into her garage in Anaheim late Tuesday evening, looking for her laundry. Instead, she found two baby opossums eating the cat food. She quickly took a stick and tried to shoo away the hungry eaters.

The babies were surprised but would not leave, so Cynthia had to poke at them and scare them away. Ms. Hachey reported that at least she was glad that she found out who had been ripping open her bags of cat food. It wasn't her naughty cats after all! She plans to keep her side door closed from now on.

Questions:

1. Who was involved?
2. What happened?
3. Where did it happen?
4. When did it happen?
5. Why did it happen?

Recommendations:

How can the author make the article more interesting?

How can the author make the article more concise?

How can the author make the article more believable?

Should any words be added or deleted?

Should any events be added or deleted?

News Article Sample
(Final Draft)

• Mealtime Marsupials •

Student Author: Stephanie Hachey

Last Tuesday evening, Cynthia Hachey walked into her garage on Eileen Drive looking for her laundry. Instead, she found two baby opossums feasting on her cat food. The Anaheim housewife picked up a pole and tried to shoo away the hungry connoisseurs.

The foot-long baby marsupials were stunned, but slow to leave, perhaps "playing possum." A swift nudge of the pole scared them out the open side door. The mystery of the torn cat food bags was finally solved, and the resident cats were no longer accused of being the culprits.

The Orange County Animal Shelter says these nocturnal marsupials are a harmless, if bothersome, common occurrence in the county. These animals are only looking for any kind of food. To keep them away, eliminate all outdoor food, including pet food.

Name: ______________________

News Article Frame

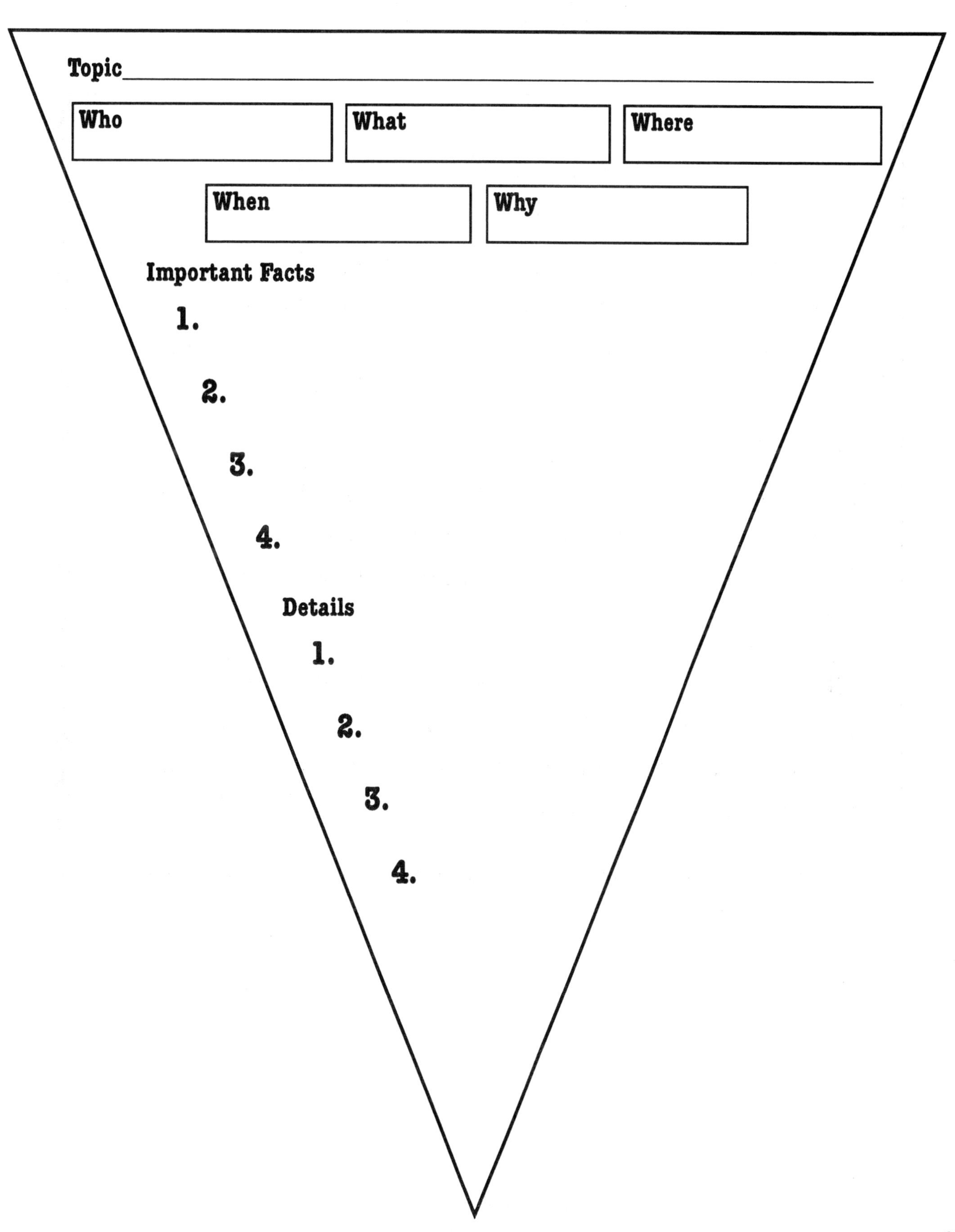

Writer's Name: ______________________ Evaluator's Name: ______________________

News Article Rubric

	Great!	O.K.	Needs Help
Critical Components			
Includes a headline or title that grabs the reader's attention			
Includes the writer's name in a byline that follows the headline			
Answers the questions *who, what, where, when,* and *why*			
Most important information comes first			
Details follow the most important information			
Includes information sources			
Style			
Word Choice			
Strong, active verbs			
Precise words			
Words that evoke imagery and sensory detail			
Coherence			
Clearly presented ideas			
Logically sequenced ideas			
Mechanics			
Ending punctuation			
Capitalization			
Comma rules			
Quotation marks			
Paragraph structure			

Comments

____

____

____

Travel Brochure

Critical Components

A travel brochure contains factual information about a specific place and attempts to entice the reader to visit the place. The information in a brochure is presented in a concise manner. A brochure includes maps, graphics, or photographs to enhance the text. (Note: Travel brochures incorporate components common to both persuasive and informative writing. While the brochure's text is intended to persuade the reader, its content must be factual and accurate. The focus of this lesson is on researching and presenting this factual content.)

Preparation

Obtain brochures that provide information about national parks, zoos, or amusement parks. Bring these to class on the day of the lesson. Photocopy pages 34–37 for students.

Setting the Stage

Display the brochures you collected. Discuss with students places of interest they have visited, such as zoos, museums, national parks, and amusement parks. Ask students whether or not they obtained brochures before or during their visit. Invite students who collected brochures to describe how the brochures helped them during their visit and made their trip more enjoyable. For example, a student may have visited an amusement park and used a brochure to find his or her way around the park and to learn about show times and other scheduled events. Finally, divide the class into small groups and give each group one of the brochures to read and study.

Instructional Input

1. After groups have had a few minutes to read their brochures, list the following headings on the board in chart format: *Location, Climate and Natural Surroundings, Historical Background,* and *Areas of Interest.* Invite groups to add under each heading appropriate information they obtained from their brochures.

2. Ask students to examine their brochures again to find examples of important information presented in a few words. Discuss with students the importance of succinct, precise writing.

3. Invite students to analyze how maps, pictures, or illustrations add to the effectiveness of their brochures. Have groups share their findings with the class.

Guided Practice

1. Provide each pair of students with a copy of the Travel Brochure Sample (Basic Research) on page 34. Discuss where the author might have obtained her information (encyclopedia, library book, and/or first-hand visit). Invite students to read and categorize the information according to the directions on the page.

2. Provide each pair of students with a copy of the Travel Brochure Format (page 36). Invite students to develop an illustrated brochure based on the Travel Brochure Sample's research.

Independent Practice

1. Have students research a place of interest and organize their research using the Travel Brochure Frame (page 35).

2. Invite students to use their completed frame as a reference in developing their own brochure or completing the Travel Brochure Format (page 36).

3. Invite students to use the Travel Brochure Rubric (page 37) and work with a partner to revise, edit, and illustrate their brochures.

Presentation

- Invite students to create an oral presentation based on the information in their brochures. These presentations can be shared in small groups or with the whole class.
- Invite each student to create a diorama depicting the location he or she researched. Brochures can be displayed next to the dioramas or attached to the side or back of the box.
- Invite students to create a brochure on a blank overhead transparency. This can be displayed to the entire class and can serve as a prompt for an oral presentation.
- If the appropriate equipment is available, invite students to create their brochures using multimedia computer programs or digital cameras.

Teaching Hints/Extensions

- Coordinate this writing assignment with a social studies unit, encouraging students to create brochures about a state, county, country, or era your class is currently studying.
- Coordinate this activity with a lesson on writing business letters. Invite students to write to various states or agencies to obtain additional research information before they create the rough draft of their brochures.

Name: ______________________________

Travel Brochure Sample
(Basic Research)

Directions: Read the following information about Yellowstone National Park. Decide how you would organize this information into a brochure format. Label each paragraph *place of interest, climate and natural surroundings,* or *historical background.*

• Yellowstone National Park •

Student Author: Kelly Russell

When Jim Bridger, Joe Meek, Warren Angus Ferris, and Osborne Russell talked and wrote about the wonders they saw at Yellowstone, no one believed them. Fountains that shot water high into the air, bubbling pools of colored mud, and smoking earth just couldn't be possible. When the wonders of Yellowstone reached the U.S. Congress, voters gave the area legal protection. On March 1, 1872, President Ulysses S. Grant signed a bill that made Yellowstone the world's first national park.

The famous geyser known as Old Faithful blows its top every 40 to 100 minutes, and it erupts more regularly than any other geyser. It shoots a four-minute spout of water from 100 to 184 feet into the air.

Elk, moose, and bison roam Yellowstone. Some bull moose weigh up to 900 pounds or more. There are also black bears and grizzly bears. Water birds vary from geese and gulls to ospreys.

Yellowstone Canyon was cut by the Yellowstone River over thousands of years. It is 24 miles long and 1,200 feet deep. Two of the park's most beautiful permanent waterfalls are in the canyon.

Yellowstone Lake is the biggest glacial lake in the park. It has 110 miles of shoreline and, in some places, it is 390 feet deep. It is so wide you can hardly see from one side to the other.

Plants in Yellowstone National Park include sagebrush, sedge, and wildflowers. Trees are numerous and include aspen, evergreen, and lodgepole pines.

Name: ____________________

Travel Brochure Frame

Directions: Record the name and location of the place of interest. Then, research and record facts about the historical background, climate and natural surroundings, and areas of interest. Write a topic sentence for each category. On a separate piece of paper, develop each paragraph in full.

Place Name: ____________________

Location: ____________________

Historical Background

Topic Sentence: ____________________

____

____

____

Facts

1.

2.

3.

Climate and Natural Surroundings

Topic Sentence: ____________________

____

____

____

Facts

1.

2.

3.

Areas of Interest

Topic Sentence: ____________________

____

____

____

Facts

1.

2.

3.

Name: ______________________________

Travel Brochure Format

Historical Background

Climate and Natural Surroundings

Areas of Interest

Writer's Name: ______________________ Evaluator's Name: ______________________

Travel Brochure Rubric

	Great!	O.K.	Needs Help
Critical Components			
Contains factual information about a specific place			
Attempts to convince the reader to visit the place			
Includes maps, graphics, and/or photographs			
Style			
Word Choice Strong, active verbs			
Precise words			
Words that evoke imagery and sensory detail			
Writing devices such as alliteration, metaphor, simile, onomatopoeia, and personification			
Originality			
Mechanics			
Ending punctuation			
Capitalization			
Comma rules			
Quotation marks			
Paragraph structure			

Comments

____

____

____

____

____

Interview

Critical Components

An interview is a way of obtaining information about a person or a specific topic. It consists of a series of questions that answer *who, what, where, when,* and *why.* Interview questions are open-ended rather than yes-or-no. Interview questions fall into one of three categories: ice-breakers, fact-finders, and in-depth probes. A written interview includes the names of the interviewee and interviewer and the date and location of the interview.

Preparation

Prepare two sets of interview questions. The first should consist of questions that can be answered with a simple *yes* or *no.* The second interview should consist of open-ended questions that serve as ice-breakers, fact-finders and in-depth probes. Make an overhead transparency of page 41. Photocopy pages 42–44 for students.

Setting the Stage

Conduct each of your prepared interviews with a student volunteer. After the interviews, ask the class to name differences between the types of questions in the two interviews. Be sure to discuss the importance of formulating and sequencing questions to provide in-depth coverage of the subject.

Instructional Input

1. Discuss the yes-or-no questions you asked in the first interview. Brainstorm with the class how these could be reworded to yield more detailed information.

2. Write several other yes-or-no questions on the board. Invite students to work with a partner to rewrite the questions into an open-ended format that would obtain a detailed response.

Examples:

Yes-or-No Question:
Do you like skateboarding?

Open-ended Question:
What aspect of skateboarding do you like the best?

Yes-or-No Question:
Do you enjoy eating spaghetti?

Open-ended Question:
What Italian foods do you like best and why?

3. Display the Interview Question Categories transparency (page 41). Discuss these three categories and their purposes. Note that probing questions may bring up sensitive issues such as fears or embarrassing personal experiences. Ice-breakers and fact-finders help set the interviewee at ease before he or she is asked more probing and sensitive questions. When sequencing the interview questions, follow the set of probing questions with a less sensitive question at the end so that the final question in the interview is more comfortable for the interviewee.

4. Distribute to students copies of the Interview Sample (page 42). Invite students to read the interview and answer the accompanying questions.

Guided Practice

1. Write on index cards descriptions of jobs such as animal trainer, sports broadcaster, actor, and stunt pilot.

2. Divide the class into groups of two or three. Have each group select a job card and write the name of the job at the top of a piece of paper.

3. Ask each group to fold their paper into thirds and label the sections *Ice-Breakers, Fact-Finders,* and *Probes.* Have them write one question they could ask the person on the card in each of the three sections.

4. Have students pass their papers from group to group. Ask the groups to write a new question under each category each time they receive a new paper.

5. Ask group members to name the job on their paper and share several of the students' questions after the papers have been passed to each group.

Independent Practice

1. Distribute to students copies of the Interview Frame (page 43). Assign each student a partner. Have students use the frame to develop questions to ask their partners, to conduct the interview, and to record the main points of their partners' answers.

2. Ask students to recopy their interviews and use their notes in developing complete sentences through which they will report their partners' responses. Have each student show the completed interview to his or her partner so the partner can check for accuracy.

3. Have students use the Interview Rubric (page 44) to assist the editing and revision of the interview.

Presentation

- Invite students to conduct their interviews in a talk-show format. Have them take turns serving as the celebrity host conducting the interviews they developed with their partners.

- Encourage students to write newspaper articles that integrate the information from their interviews with the skills they learned in the previous lesson.

Teaching Hints/Extensions

- Provide at an interview center pictures of people involved in careers such as architect, farmer, musician, teacher, doctor, parent, artist, and athlete. Invite students to work in pairs, with one student assuming the role of a person in one of the pictures and the other interviewing him or her about the career.

- Invite students to create interview questions for fictional characters, such as Matt from *Sign of the Beaver* or Karana from *Island of the Blue Dolphins,* or historical characters such as Florence Nightingale and Thomas Edison. This is a fun way to reinforce literature, history, and science content.

- During holiday celebrations, invite students to conduct interviews that provide insight into important celebrations. Topics can include real or legendary characters or inanimate objects such as the Chanukah menorah, Christmas tree, or Kwanzaa kinara. Let students suggest the roles so that the interviews reflect your classroom population. Have students exchange papers and write answers to their partner's questions, or have them interview each other aloud.

- Invite a school staff member such as the librarian, nurse, or custodian to visit your classroom. Prior to the visit, have students develop interview questions. Encourage students to take notes as they talk with the staff member and later compile their findings into a written interview.

Interview Question Categories

ICE-BREAKERS

Ice-breakers are designed to put people at ease. They do not necessarily relate to the topic you will be discussing. They are often a subject of mutual interest.

Examples:
How long have you lived in Chicago?
Did you attend the last Cubs game?

FACT-FINDERS

These questions relate to the subject you will be discussing. They address the five journalistic questions: *who, what, where, when,* and *why.*

Examples:
Why did you become a police officer?
What kind of training did you receive?

PROBES

These questions dig deeper than basic fact-finders. They are asked in order to reveal an insight or response that will provide a deeper level of understanding about the topic.

Examples:
What is the most frightening aspect of your job and how do you conquer your fear?
What is the most rewarding aspect of your job? Why?

Name: ______________________________

Interview Sample

Student Author: Tawny Cahill

Interview with Kay Bass, Founder and Former Owner of Katie McGuire's Pie Shops
December 20, 1997
Fullerton, California

Q: You once owned a chain of pie shops. I guess the obvious question is, do you love pies?

A: Yes, I sure do!

Q: What's your favorite kind of pie?

A: I love homemade apple pie hot from the oven.

Q: When did you first become interested in opening a pie shop?

A: I started thinking about opening a pie shop in 1982. The exciting day that I opened my first shop was in February, 1984.

Q: Where was your first shop located?

A: My first shop was located on Balboa Island, near my home.

Q: Did you hire family members to help out when your pie shop opened?

A: In the beginning, most of the family would come and help out when the shop got busy. Everyone was wonderful about helping out before we could afford employees.

Q: How did you come up with the name "Katie McGuire's"?

A: I wanted the name to be old-fashioned, so I made inquiries. My middle name is Katie, so I finally came up with "Katie McGuire's."

Q: How many pie stores did you eventually own?

A: I had 26 lovely stores all around Southern California.

Q: How many years did you invest in Katie McGuire's?

A: I put 15 wonderful years into Katie McGuire's. I sold the chain this year.

Q: Did it hurt you to sell your pie shops?

A: It was sad, but it was time to devote my time and energy to my family.

Q: What are you doing now?

A: I'm working with my husband building an insurance company.

Q: What were the most satisfying aspects of owning Katie McGuire's?

A: Having satisfied customers and watching the shops grow.

Questions:

1. What questions did the interviewer ask to "break the ice"?
2. Which questions do you consider "in-depth probes"?

Name: ______________________________

Interview Frame

Person Interviewed: ______________________________

Date of Interview: ______________________________

Location of Interview: ______________________________

Directions:

1. Choose subjects such as hobbies, special interests, family and friends, sports, and future plans to discuss during your interview.
2. Develop ice-breaker, fact-finder, and in-depth probe questions to ask about these subjects.
3. Conduct the interview, making notes about the main points of your interviewee's answers.
4. Rewrite the questions and answers on a separate sheet of paper in complete sentences. Show this completed interview to your interviewee to check for accuracy.

ICE-BREAKERS

Q: ______________________________

A: ______________________________

Q: ______________________________

A: ______________________________

FACT-FINDERS

Q: ______________________________

A: ______________________________

Q: ______________________________

A: ______________________________

IN-DEPTH PROBES

Q: ______________________________

A: ______________________________

Q: ______________________________

A: ______________________________

Writer's Name: ______________________ Evaluator's Name: ______________________

Interview Rubric

	Great!	O.K.	Needs Help
Critical Components			
Addresses *who, what, where, when,* and *why*			
Includes open-ended questions that cannot be answered with *yes* or *no*			
Includes three categories of questions: ice-breakers, fact-finders, and in-depth probes			
Includes the names of the interviewee and interviewer, and the date and location of the interview			
Style			
Word Choice			
Strong, active verbs			
Precise words			
Coherence			
Clearly presented ideas			
Logically sequenced ideas			
Originality			
Mechanics			
Ending punctuation			
Capitalization			
Comma rules			
Quotation marks			
Paragraph structure			

Comments

____

____

____

Survey

Critical Components

A survey elicits information about a group of people. A survey consists of a series of related questions. Survey questions have multiple-choice answers. Lists of multiple-choice answers include a "catchall" choice, such as *all of the above, none of the above,* or *other.* Summaries of survey results include specific descriptions of the population sampled and answers to *who, what, where, when,* and *why.* Survey results are summarized in a variety of formats, including narratives, pie graphs, bar graphs, and pictographs.

Preparation

Make overhead transparencies of pages 51 and 52. Photocopy pages 53–57 for students.

Setting the Stage

Stimulate interest in surveys by asking students to predict which pet they think would be the class favorite if students were asked to choose between cats, dogs, hamsters, and birds. After students make their predictions on a slip of paper, survey the class and tally the results. After making the tally, summarize the results for the students. For example, *15 out of 30, or 50% of the class, chose dogs as their favorite pet. 10 out of 30, or 33% of the class, chose cats as their favorite pet.* Ask students to compare their predictions with the survey.

Establish the importance of surveys. Surveying your population is a helpful way to make marketing decisions. For example, finding out which pets are the most popular in the local area helps a pet-store owner make knowledgeable purchases for the store. If the store owner knows the market well, he or she may be able to use a survey to predict which pets will sell best.

Another important purpose of surveys is that they give a person the ability to report general tendencies. For example, a writer of the results of an opinion poll might make statements such as *most of the population feels that the governor made an unwise decision* or *the majority of the population agrees with the governor's decision.* This type of data is very helpful in informational writing (as well as in persuasive writing).

Instructional Input

1. Explain that there are several steps to successfully conducting a survey. Use the overhead transparency of page 51 to give a brief overview of the "Six Steps to Survey Success." (A detailed explanation of each step is included in the Guided Practice and Independent Practice sections of this lesson.)

SIX STEPS TO SURVEY SUCCESS

1. Define the survey topic.
2. Define the audience.
3. Write the survey.
4. Practice conducting the survey.
5. Conduct the survey and record the results.
6. Summarize and report the results.

2. Use the overhead transparency of the Survey Sample (page 52) to show students how the author approached the survey process. First, she decided she was curious about people's "favorites." She brainstormed a list of favorites and wrote this survey. Read the survey aloud to the class.

3. As the author conducted the survey, she tallied the subjects' opinions. Orally administer this same survey to your class. Record responses on the overhead projector to demonstrate the technique for tallying results.

4. After the author finished conducting the survey, she determined the percentage of people selecting each choice by dividing the number of people responding to the choice by the total number of people in the survey. She then summarized the results. Distribute copies of this summary, the Survey Results sample (page 53).

5. Explain how graphs are useful visuals for enhancing the communication of a survey's results. Discuss how the pie graphs enhance the presentation of the Survey Sample's results and distribute to students copies of page 54 (Showing the Information) to introduce them to other graphic options. Have students practice interpreting these graphs.

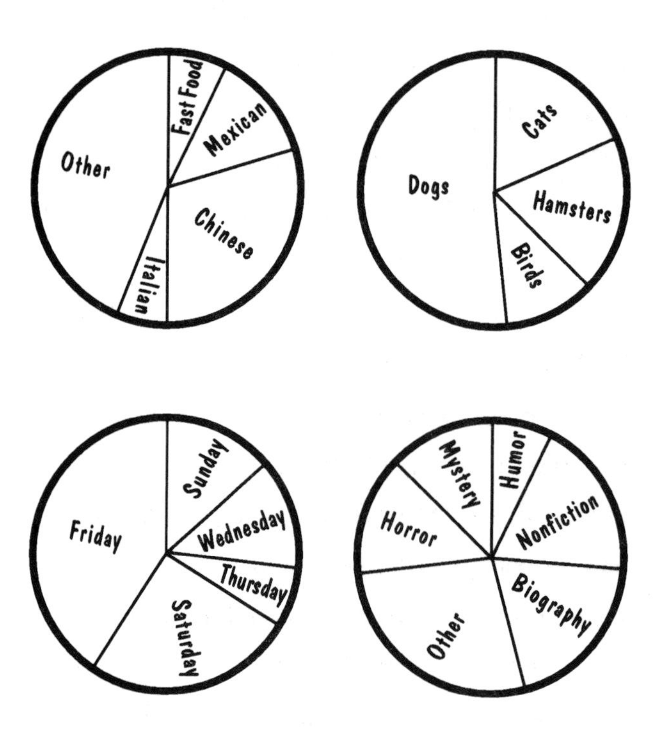

6. Have students read the Writing Survey Results reproducible (page 55) to learn various ways of reporting the findings of each item's responses. Have students practice writing results from various perspectives.

Guided Practice

Guide students through the first four steps of the survey-writing process and have them use the Survey Frame (page 56) for assistance. (The fifth and sixth steps are covered in the Independent Practice section.)

1. Define the survey topic.

Brainstorm and record on the board general topics such as sports, music, and art. Ask each student to settle on a different topic.

2. Define the audience.

Ask each student to choose a population to survey (e.g., boys, girls, fourth graders, sixth graders, adults, students at their school, people in their city). Remind students that they must have access to the people they will survey.

3. Write the survey.

Encourage students to limit their first survey to three or four questions. Show them how subtopics for their main topic lend themselves to becoming individual items on a survey. Caution students to avoid overlap in their subtopics. For example, consider the subtopics under each of the following main topics:

Sports	**Art**
stars teams sports	artists famous artworks media
Music	**Favorites**
composers compositions instruments	pets foods books

If a student chooses "Art," he or she could develop from the subtopics survey questions such as the following:

Who is your favorite artist?
What is your favorite artwork?
What is your favorite art medium?

After developing the questions, students need to develop possible responses and a general option for responses that do not fall into any of the available options. For example:

Who is your favorite artist?

a. Michelangelo
b. DaVinci
c. Monet
d. Van Gogh
e. other

What is your favorite artwork?

a. Michelangelo's *David*
b. DaVinci's *Last Supper*
c. Monet's *Water Lilies*
d. Van Gogh's *Irises*
e. other

What is your favorite art medium?

a. sculpture
b. oil
c. watercolor
d. pen and ink
e. other

Naturally, the more experience your students gain in writing, conducting, and reporting surveys, the more specific their surveys will become. For example, a student might conduct his first survey on sports; however, his second survey will more than likely just relate to a single sport, such as baseball. And, for example, a student writing a survey about art quickly learns that a narrower focus (for example, on impressionist art alone) makes more sense, because it is quite difficult to compare a sculpture with an oil painting. Students may also find that, as they conduct a survey, issues may arise that demonstrate a need for more refined questions.

4. Practice conducting the survey.

After students have written their surveys, ask a student volunteer to help you model an appropriately conducted survey in front of the class. Be sure to model introductory and closing remarks. For example:

> Teacher:
> **Hello, my name is ________ and I am conducting a survey on music. This survey will take about one minute. May I ask you a few questions?**
>
> Student:
> **Yes**
>
> Teacher:
> **(Ask the questions.)**
>
> Student:
> **(Answer the questions.)**
>
> Teacher:
> **Thank you for your time.**

If the potential survey subject declines, students should kindly thank the person and wish him or her a nice day.

After modeling an appropriate survey, ask a few students to rehearse in front of the class. Gently correct them and help them with cordial introductions and closings. Then, have students pair off in partners for practice. Introducing themselves to a person they don't know and explaining the purpose of the survey is generally more challenging than actually conducting the survey.

Independent Practice

5. Conduct the survey and record the results.

Encourage students to conduct their surveys during lunch or recess, or in class, depending on their audience. Remind them to tally the results as they give their survey. Require a minimum pool of 20 to 30 respondents.

6. Summarize and report the results.

Ask students to summarize their survey results using text and graphs. You may want to walk the class through writing up one student's results before letting students independently summarize their surveys. Make sure students understand the function of each type of graph before selecting one to use in their results. Some graphs are more appropriate than others for certain types of information.

Percentages are an important statistic in the narrative reporting of a survey's findings. Remind students how to convert fractions to percentages by dividing the numerator by the denominator and multiplying by 100. For example:

$$\frac{\text{number of students in favor of smaller classes} \ldots 15}{\text{total number of students surveyed} \ldots\ldots\ldots\ldots 20}$$

$$15 \div 20 = .75$$
$$.75 \times 100 = 75\%$$

Encourage students to use the Survey Rubric (page 57) to self-, peer, and group evaluate their work.

Presentation

- Students can report results in a classroom or school newspaper. Be sure they include graphs and accompanying text. Invite students to add captions below each graph that describe the information.

- Compile student reports to make a class book titled *Room __'s Survey Responses.* Consider creating several survey books based on themes such as preference surveys, opinion surveys, or activity surveys. Submit an extra copy of these books to your school library.

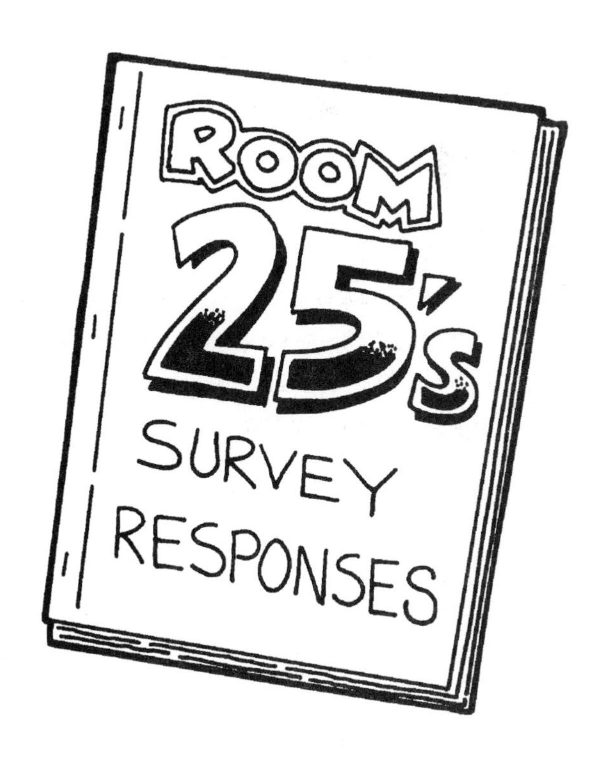

- Post results on a bulletin board titled *Survey Responses.* Heighten the visual interest by helping students create pictographs, photographs, drawings, and mini-articles that complement and enhance the information on the display.

Teaching Tips/Extensions

- Help students expand their writing skills by having them integrate the results of one of their surveys into a news article or brochure. For example, a student may wish to include the results of a survey about the popularity of a vacation spot when creating a travel brochure for that location.

- Encourage students to integrate science content into their survey writing skills. Instead of surveying people, invite them to examine nature. For example, if they were studying tree damage, they might examine each tree for damage related to smog, insects, fire, drought, or overwatering. Have them scientifically observe nearby trees, tally results, and report their findings.

Six Steps to Survey Success

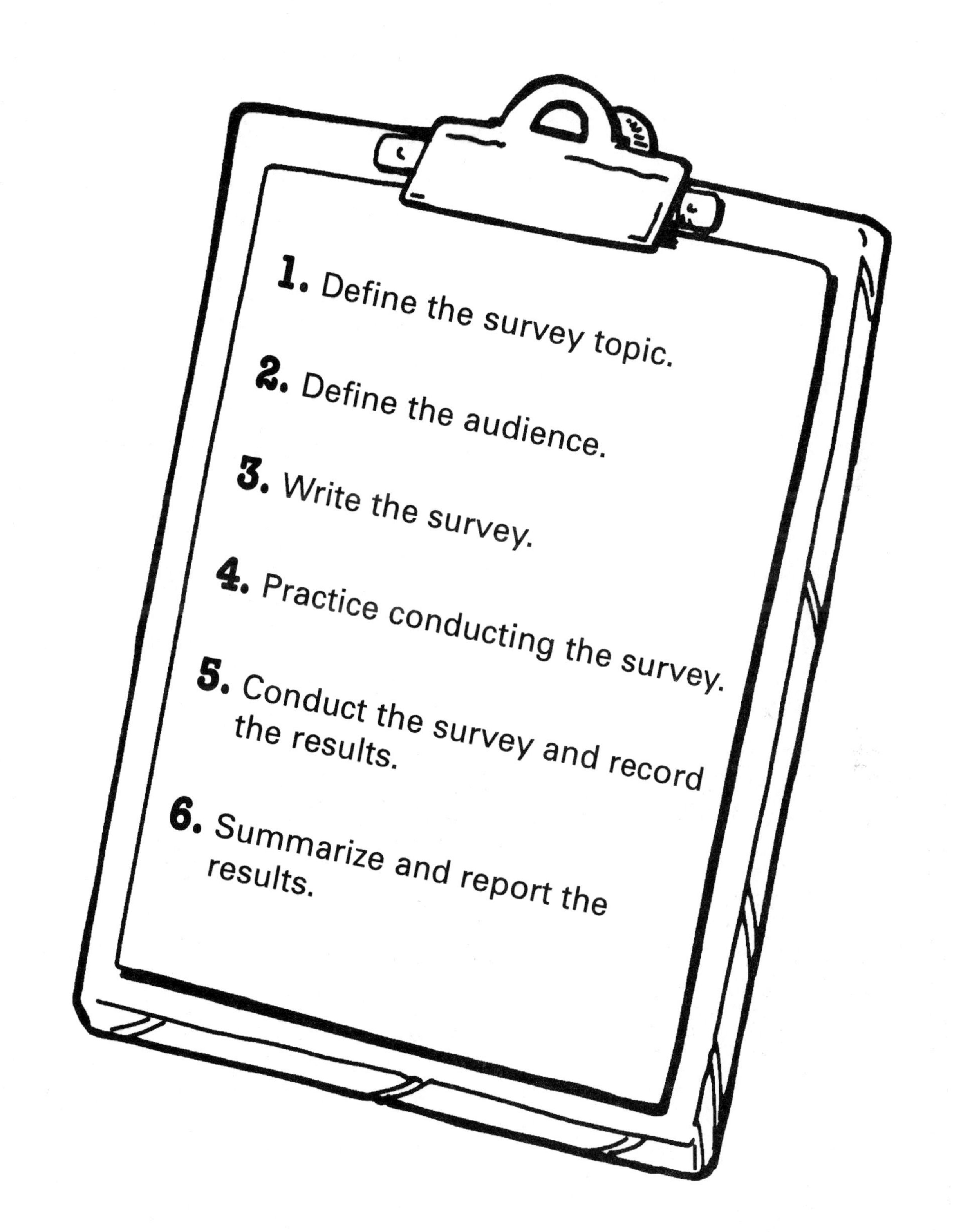

Survey Sample

Favorites Survey

Student Author: Shaheema Shaw

1. What is your favorite pet?

a. dog
b. cat
c. hamster
d. bird
e. other

2. What is your favorite food?

a. fast food
b. Italian food
c. Chinese food
d. Japanese food
e. Mexican food
f. other

3. What is your favorite type of book?

a. horror
b. mystery
c. humor
d. nonfiction
e. biography
f. other

4. What is your favorite day of the week?

a. Monday
b. Tuesday
c. Wednesday
d. Thursday
e. Friday
f. Saturday
g. Sunday

Name: ______________________________

Survey Results

Student Author: Shaheema Shaw

I was curious about people's favorites so I surveyed 30 adults and children of all ages at my school. I gave the survey in mid-December 1997, in Orange County, California. Here is what I found out.

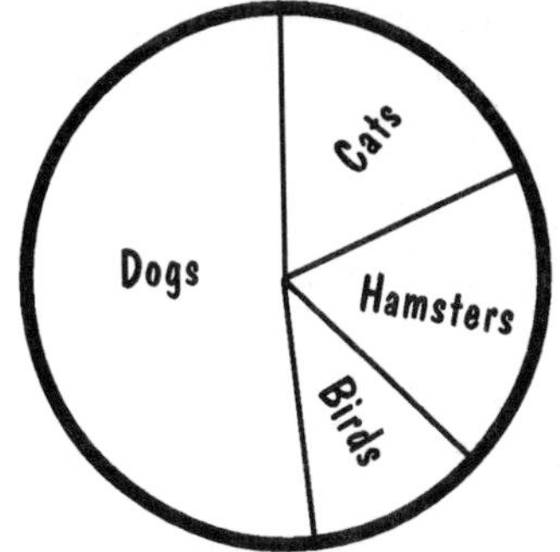

Votes for favorite pets were as follows: 53% liked dogs, 20% liked cats, 20% liked hamsters, and 7% liked birds.

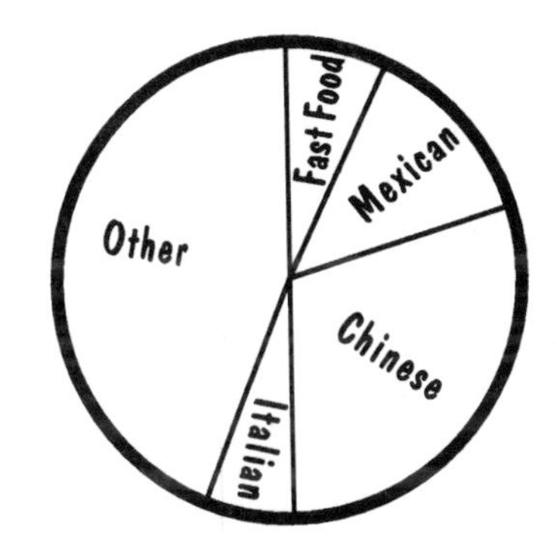

People's favorite foods were: 7% fast food, 13% Mexican food, 6% Italian food, 27% Chinese food. There were no votes for Japanese food. 46% of the people voted for other types of food.

Votes for favorite books were: 13% liked horror, 13% liked mystery, 7% liked humor, 20% liked nonfiction, and 20% liked biography. 27% liked types of books not listed on the survey.

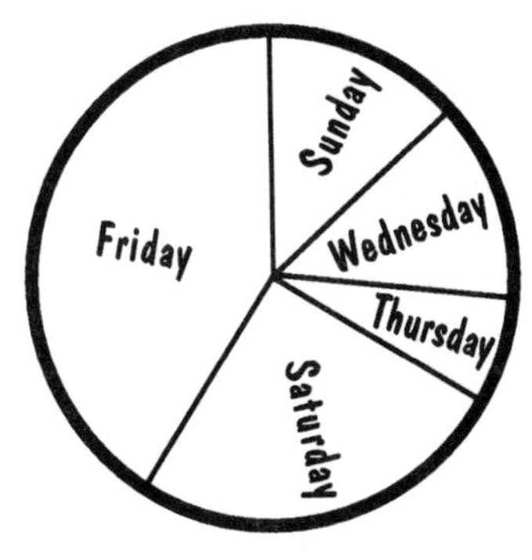

When I asked, "What is your favorite day of the week?" no one answered Monday or Tuesday. 13% liked Wednesday and 13% liked Sunday. Only 7% liked Thursday. 40% of the people liked Friday and 27% liked Saturday.

Discussion:

1. Does the first paragraph answer the five key journalistic questions? Identify the answers.

2. Do the category percentages add up to 100%? Were any numbers rounded up or down? If so, which numbers?

3. Are the results reported succinctly and in an interesting fashion? Give two examples.

Name: ______________________________

Showing the Information

Votes for favorite pets were as follows: 16 people liked dogs, 6 people liked cats, 6 people liked hamsters, and 2 people liked birds.

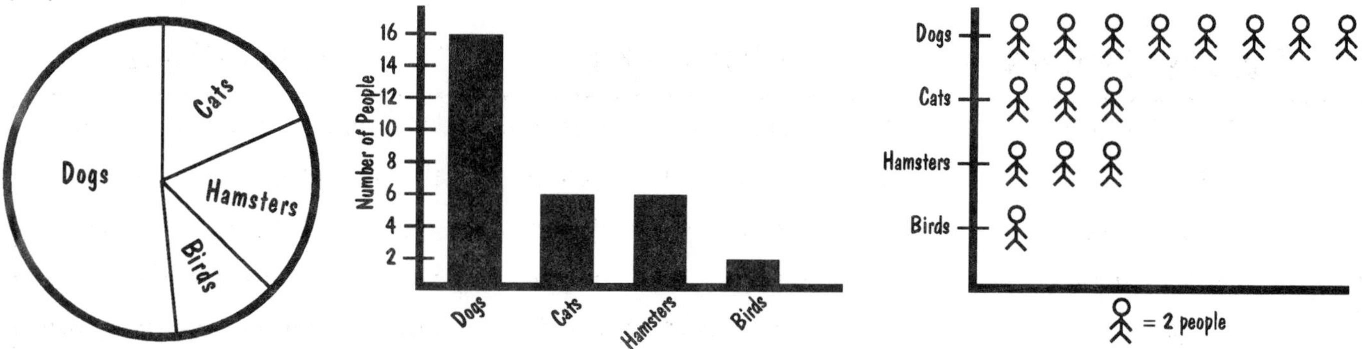

Votes for favorite books were: 4 people liked horror, 4 people liked mystery, 2 people liked humor, 6 people liked nonfiction, 6 people liked biography, and 8 people liked types of books not listed on the survey.

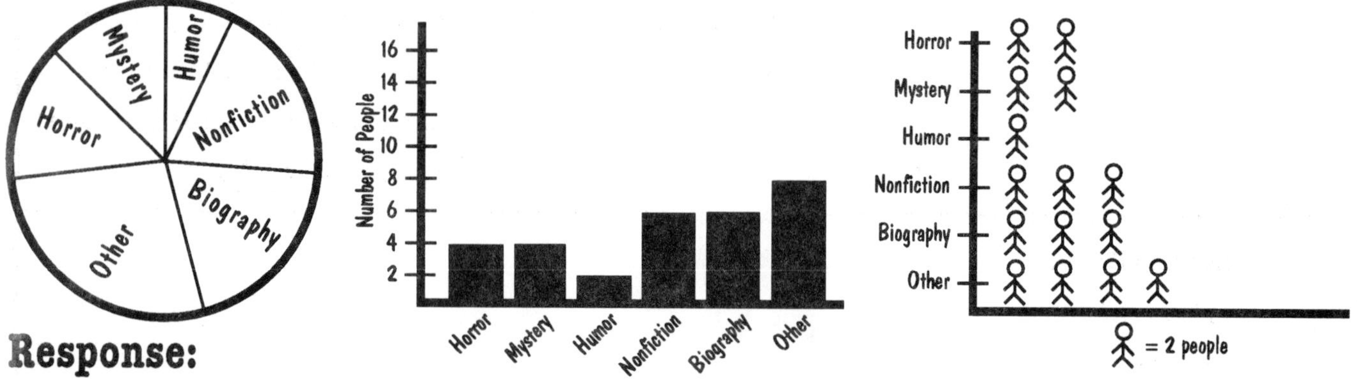

Response:

1. Which type of graph is most appealing to you and why?

2. Which type of graph will you use to illustrate your survey's findings and why?

Exercise:

Create a pie chart, bar graph, and pictograph illustrating the information below.

When I asked, "What is your favorite day of the week?" no one answered Monday or Tuesday. 4 people liked Wednesday and 4 people liked Sunday. Only 2 people liked Thursday. 12 people liked Friday and 8 liked Saturday.

Name: ______________________________

Writing Survey Results

Directions: Study the examples and then write in the blank boxes four paragraphs from various perspectives.

Survey Results	Write-Up 1	Write-Up 2
Favorite Pets 53% dogs 20% cats 20% hamsters 7% birds 0% other	A recent survey indicates that dogs, by far, are the favorite American pet. This data supports the old adage "dog is man's best friend." Votes for favorite pets were as follows: 53% liked dogs, 20% liked cats, 20% liked hamsters, and 7% liked birds.	Dispelling the recent rumor that hamsters are not well-liked pets, my recent survey indicates that a significant portion of the population likes them! Though 80% of the population do favor other types of pets, I am pleased to report that 20% of the population sampled prefer hamsters over dogs, cats, and birds!
Favorite Books 13% horror 13% mystery 7% humor 20% nonfiction 20% biography 27% other		
Favorite Day of the Week 0% Monday 0% Tuesday 13% Wednesday 7% Thursday 40% Friday 27% Saturday 13% Sunday		

Name: ______________________________

Survey Frame

Step One: What is your topic? ____

Step Two: What are your basic questions and responses?

Question 1:

Responses
a.
b.
c.
d.
e. other

Question 2:

Responses
a.
b.
c.
d.
e. other

Question 3:

Responses
a.
b.
c.
d.
e. other

Question 4:

Responses
a.
b.
c.
d.
e. other

Step Three: How will you report the results? (Circle at least one)

Summary Bar Graph Pie Graph Line Graph

Writer's Name: ______________________ Evaluator's Name: ______________________

Survey Rubric

	Great!	O.K.	Needs Help
Critical Components			
Gathers information from a group of people			
Consists of a series of related questions			
Questions have multiple-choice answers			
Answer choices include a "catchall"			
Summary of results includes specific descriptions of the population sampled and answers *who, what, where, when,* and *why*			
Numbers are accurately and appropriately summarized in formats such as percentages, pie graphs, bar graphs, and pictographs			
Style			
Word Choice Strong, active verbs			
Precise words			
Coherence Clearly presented ideas			
Logically sequenced ideas			
Originality			
Mechanics			
Ending punctuation			
Capitalization			
Comma rules			
Quotation marks			
Paragraph structure			

How-To

Critical Components

How-tos contain specific direction words *(north, south, east, west; stir, bake, fry, boil; left, right, up, down)*. How-tos are written with concise words and phrases. How-tos are often written in a step-by-step format. How-tos often include exact numbers (amounts, measurements, time, temperature).

Preparation

Collect examples of "how-to" writing, such as recipes, directions for traveling to particular locations, and directions for assembling a model. Write directions for discovering a "treasure" (a bag of candy, trinkets, or small toys) hidden in the classroom. Roll up the directions and insert them into a bottle. Photocopy pages 61–63 for students.

Setting the Stage

When students come in from recess, explain to them that you have discovered some directions to a hidden treasure in the classroom. Ask for three student volunteers to follow the directions to solve this mystery. Have one student read the directions aloud to the class, one student make the decisions as to how to follow the directions (for example, this student would decide which way is north or make required measurements), and one student move along the path decided upon. Instruct the rest of the class to quietly observe.

Your directions might include the following:

1. *Enter at the south door.*
2. *Walk one yard west.*
3. *Turn left.*
4. *Walk three yards north.*
5. *Turn east.*
6. *Walk seven and a half feet.*
7. *Look for a brown bag two and a half feet off the floor.*
8. *Find the treasure inside the brown bag.*
9. *Share the treasure with the class.*

If the treasure is not discovered because students incorrectly follow the directions, repeat the procedure with new volunteers.

Once the treasure has been discovered and shared, discuss the following questions:

Why is following directions important? (Following directions saves the reader time and helps him or her successfully complete the task.)

Why must directions be precise? (Precise directions help the reader understand the steps and complete the task correctly.)

What role do numbers play in directions? (Numbers give precise measurements of time, materials, space, and temperature.)

Discuss the application and importance of how-to writing in computer manuals, car maintenance manuals, appliance instructions, teacher's manuals, and cookbooks.

Instructional Input

1. Distribute copies of the How-To Sample (page 61). Ask students to listen for the critical components of how-tos as you read the passage aloud.

2. Ask students to circle and label the critical components as shown.

How to Plant a Tree

Student Author: John Hoover

To plant a tree, first go to the plant nursery and pick out a sapling [concise word] (a young, small tree) about twelve inches high [exact number]. Then, go to your backyard, or somewhere you think would look better if a tree were there, and use a rake to clear out a space of soil about as big as this page. Dig a hole with a shovel slightly deeper and wider than the base of the sapling. Place the sapling in the hole, keeping the tree upright [concise phrase]. Then, cover the hole with dirt and put a tomato cage around it so animals won't dig it up.

When the tree is approximately three feet tall, hammer eight-foot [exact number] stakes on opposite sides, about two feet into the ground. Then, take four feet of heavy-duty string and cut it in half. Next, take one end of one of the halves and tie it around the stake on the right. Then, take the other end and tie it firmly to the tree. Repeat on the left side [concise phrase]. Leave the stakes in until the tree is about six inches thick [exact number]. In about 30 years, you'll have a big, healthy tree.

3. Discuss how the key to effective how-to writing is the ability to break down a task into its component parts and then to communicate these steps clearly to the reader.

Guided Practice

1. Ask students to write out the steps for tying shoelaces. Give them about two minutes. At first, students may think it will be easy, and then they will quickly realize just how difficult it is to choose precise words.

2. Ask a few students to read the beginning of their directions. Record these openings on the board and help the writers refine the directions to simpler language.

3. Ask students to write directions for a second task, such as how to brush teeth. Give them about five minutes. Students usually find the task a little easier the second time.

4. Ask student volunteers to read their "How to Brush Your Teeth" passages. As you listen, ask questions such as *When did you tell the reader to put the toothpaste on the toothbrush? Did you tell the reader which direction to brush? Did you tell the reader to rinse?*

Independent Practice

1. Share with your students that a common cause of failure in how-to writing is leaving out steps normally considered insignificant.

2. Distribute copies of the How-To Frame (page 62).

3. Ask each student to choose a how-to topic that interests him or her. Possibilities include *How to Wash Your Dog, How to Plant a Garden, How to Care for a Pet Snake,* and *How to Make Pancakes.*

4. Ask students to list the main steps of their how-to on the frame. Then, ask them to insert additional steps between the major steps as needed. As time goes on, students can enlarge the frame to fit the needs of their topic.

5. After students list the main steps, have them combine the steps into an appropriate format, such as a numbered list of directions, a narrative, or a recipe.

6. Distribute the How-To Rubric (page 63) for self-, peer, and group evaluations during the steps of the writing process.

Presentation

- Compile the how-tos into a class publication with chapter divisions by topic. For example, your publication may have chapters titled *Mechanical How-Tos, Nature How-Tos, Recipes,* or *Building Projects.*

- Design a bulletin board titled *How-To Hints* that displays students' how-to writings.

Teaching Hints/Extensions

- Combine how-to writing with content areas. For example, have students write how-tos for long division, multiplication, or fractions. Have them publish these how-tos in a file box where they can access cards as needed. Or, have students write how-tos for successful science experiments. Save these for years of handy lesson-planning reference.

Name: ______________________________

How-To Sample

How to Plant a Tree

Student Author: John Hoover

To plant a tree, first go to the plant nursery and pick out a sapling (a young, small tree) about twelve inches high. Then, go to your backyard, or somewhere you think would look better if a tree were there, and use a rake to clear out a space of soil about as big as this page. Dig a hole with a shovel slightly deeper and wider than the base of the sapling. Place the sapling in the hole, keeping the tree upright. Then, cover the hole with dirt and put a tomato cage around it so animals won't dig it up.

When the tree is approximately three feet tall, hammer eight-foot stakes on opposite sides, about two feet into the ground. Then, take four feet of heavy-duty string and cut it in half. Next, take one end of one of the halves and tie it around the stake on the right. Then, take the other end and tie it firmly to the tree. Repeat on the left side. Leave the stakes in until the tree is about six inches thick. In about 30 years, you'll have a big, healthy tree.

Name: ___________________________

How-To Frame

Directions: List the major steps for your how-to in the left column. Then, list in the right column minor steps that occur between the major steps. (Some major steps may not need minor steps.) Continue this diagram on a separate piece of paper until all of the essential steps have been listed. After listing all of the steps, write the first draft of your how-to.

Major Steps	Minor Steps
1.	___________________________
	___________________________
	___________________________
2.	___________________________
	___________________________
	___________________________
3.	___________________________
	___________________________
	___________________________
4.	___________________________
	___________________________
	___________________________

Writer's Name: ______________________ Evaluator's Name: ______________________

How-To Rubric

	Great!	O.K.	Needs Help
Critical Components			
Contains specific direction words, such as *north, south, east, west; stir, bake, fry, boil; left, right, up, down*			
Contains words and phrases that are clear and easy to understand			
Written in a step-by-step format			
Includes exact numbers (amounts, measurements, time, temperature)			
Style			
Word Choice Strong, active verbs			
Precise words			
Number words			
Coherence Clearly presented ideas			
Logically sequenced ideas			
Originality			
Mechanics			
Ending punctuation			
Capitalization			
Comma rules			
Quotation marks			
Paragraph structure			

Comments

____

____

____

Bibliography

Batzle, Janine. *Portfolio Assessment and Evaluation.* Creative Teaching Press, 1992. How to develop and use portfolios in K–6 classrooms.

Elbow, Peter. *Writing with Power: Techniques for Mastering the Writing Process.* Oxford University Press, 1981. A self-help resource book for adults who want to improve their writing.

Flynn, Kris. *Graphic Organizers.* Creative Teaching Press, 1995. Visual aides to help children organize their thinking and writing.

Graves, Donald H. *A Fresh Look at Writing.* Heinemann, 1994. A professional writing book for teachers, with fundamentals for broadening children's writing repertoires.

McCarthy, Tara. *150 Thematic Writing Activities.* Scholastic, 1993. Reproducible reading and writing motivators for students with diverse interests and learning strengths.

Miller, Wilma H. *Alternative Assessment Techniques for Reading & Writing.* Center for Applied Research in Education, 1995. Simple and practical assessment techniques with reproducible tools.

Schifferle, Judith. *Editorial Skills.* Center for Applied Research in Education, Inc., 1985. Reproducible activities for helping students sharpen their editorial skills.

Schifferle, Judith. *Word Skills.* Center for Applied Research in Education, Inc., 1985. Reproducible activities to help students expand their writing vocabulary.

Sparks, J.E. *Write for Power.* Communication Associates, 1995. Step-by-step procedures to help strengthen children's writing.

Sunflower, Cherlyn. *Really Writing! Ready-to-Use Writing Process Activities for the Elementary Grades.* Center for Applied Research in Education, 1994. Creative writing lessons in the narrative, expressive, informative, and persuasive domains.